WITH JESUS
I am Brave

This book belongs to:

....

....

Copyrights

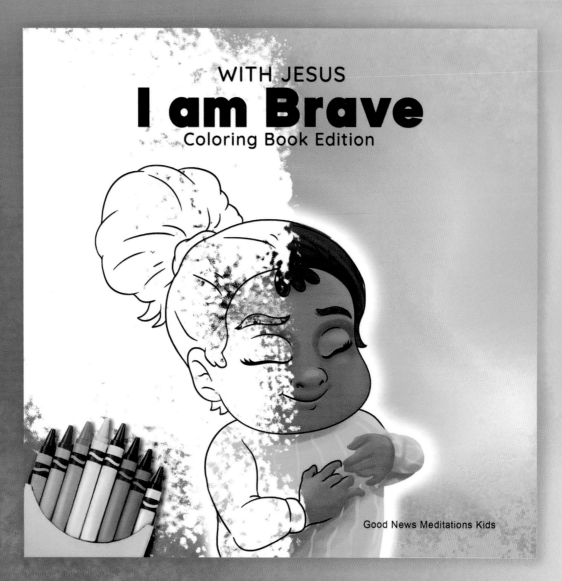

To receive print-ready samples from the coloring book version of this book, please go to gnmkids.com/free

Today, Mia had a great day. She went to the market with her mommy and played in the backyard. Now, she's brushing her teeth and getting ready to go to bed.

Daddy and Mommy come to tuck her in and pray with her. "Dear Jesus, thank you for this beautiful day. We thank you for always being with us, and we thank you for protecting us as we sleep tonight. Amen."

"Goodnight, Mia,"
Daddy and Mommy say.

"Goodnight, Mommy and
Daddy," Mia answers as
she closes her eyes to
sleep.

Suddenly, Mia feels afraid
because she can't see a thing
in the dark. She starts to shake
and screams, "Daddy! I'm scared!"

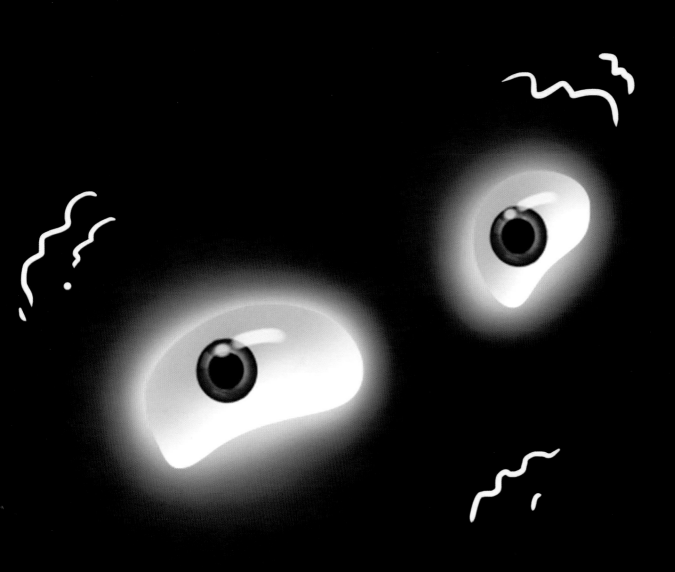

Daddy comes running into the room and asks, "What is going on, Mia?"

"It's dark in here. I can't see anything and it scares me!" Mia says.

"Don't be afraid, my dear. Close your eyes and you'll fall asleep," Daddy tells Mia. Then he closes the door.

Mia suddenly wakes up and feels afraid because it's still dark. She starts imagining things.

What if a big monster comes into my room and jumps on me?

"Daddy, I'm scared!" she screams.

Daddy comes in, sits on her bed, and says,
"Mia, you have nothing to fear
because Jesus is with you.
He has given you great courage to face anything.
When you feel afraid, say to yourself that with
Jesus you are a brave girl."

"Okay, Daddy, I will."
Mia goes back to sleep.

Suddenly, Mia starts to feel afraid
again. She's about to yell when
she remembers what her
Daddy told her.

With courage, Mia sits up straight on her bed and says, "Jesus is with me. I am brave, I am brave, I am brave!" Then she lies back down.

Mia is no longer afraid of the dark because she realizes that with Jesus, she is a brave little girl!

The End.

For God hath not given
us the spirit of fear; but of power,
and of love, and of a sound mind.

2 Timothy 1v7

Author's note:

Thank you so much for reading this book. If you enjoyed this book, we would love it if you could leave a review and recommend it to a friend.

If there is anything you would like to share with us to help us improve this book, please go to gnmkids.com/feedback

Please checkout our other books

www.gnmkids.com